Polo
the bear cub

A story of the frozen north

Written by Tim Healey
Illustrated by Nick Butterworth and Mick Inkpen

PUBLISHED BY THE READER'S DIGEST ASSOCIATION LIMITED

Polo's first memories were of the warm den. It was a cave scooped deep in the snow, and he snuggled there against his mother's fur all through the long northern winter.

One day, Polo's mother said, "We must leave now and look for food." And she tunnelled out through the soft snow which had drifted into the mouth of the den.

Polo followed his mother.
Outside, for the first time, he saw
the colours of the sky and the
pale, cold world spread beneath it.

A snowy owl flew by on silent wings. The little bear stumbled in surprise. It was the first time that Polo had really used his legs, and it took a while to get used to them.

But soon Polo was scampering happily about. Mother bear sniffed the air and led her cub off towards the sea. All the time, she watched out for danger. Once, the two of them surprised a fluffy white creature with long ears and a bobbly tail.

The creature ran off amazingly fast, and Polo asked, "Is that what danger looks like?"

His mother replied that it was only a hare, and there was no danger in it.

Later, mother noticed a white fox following them at a distance. "Is that danger?" Polo asked again. But mother replied that there was no real danger in the fox.
"I am much too strong for him," she said. "He only hopes we will find some food and leave tasty pickings behind."
All the same, mother bear growled once or twice in the fox's direction. The creature soon ran off.

Before long, Polo began to sniff exciting salty smells in the air. Then he heard the clamour of seabirds. And suddenly, for the first time, Polo saw the grey-green sea. It spread in glittering sheets, broken here and there by vast stretches of firm white ice.

In the distance, a great whale spouted. Was that danger?
Polo had no time to ask as mother led him out onto the ice.

Mother bear found a hole in the ice, and said it was a good place to catch seals.

"Seals often swim under the ice," she explained. "They can go a long time without breathing. But sooner or later they must come up for air. They are good to eat, and you can sometimes catch them as they poke their heads through these air holes."

Polo said that he would catch her
a nice fat seal for her supper.
And he waited patiently by the
hole while mother looked for
food nearby.

Polo waited

and waited.

Suddenly a seal did poke its head up through the hole. The little bear was so astonished that he could not think what to do.
The seal looked at Polo.
Polo looked at the seal,

and the seal vanished under the ice again.

Polo trotted after his mother to explain what had happened. But she did not listen closely. She was crouching low on the ice, and watching many more seals bask in the distance.

So Polo went off to play on his own. He climbed to the top of an ice bank,

and slid to the bottom with a bump.

He chased after a crowd of seabirds and watched as they flew off with loud cries.

Round the corner of one icy hillock, Polo saw part of something smooth and brown. "Mother shall have a nice fat seal for her supper," he told himself. And he crept slowly round the corner to pounce.

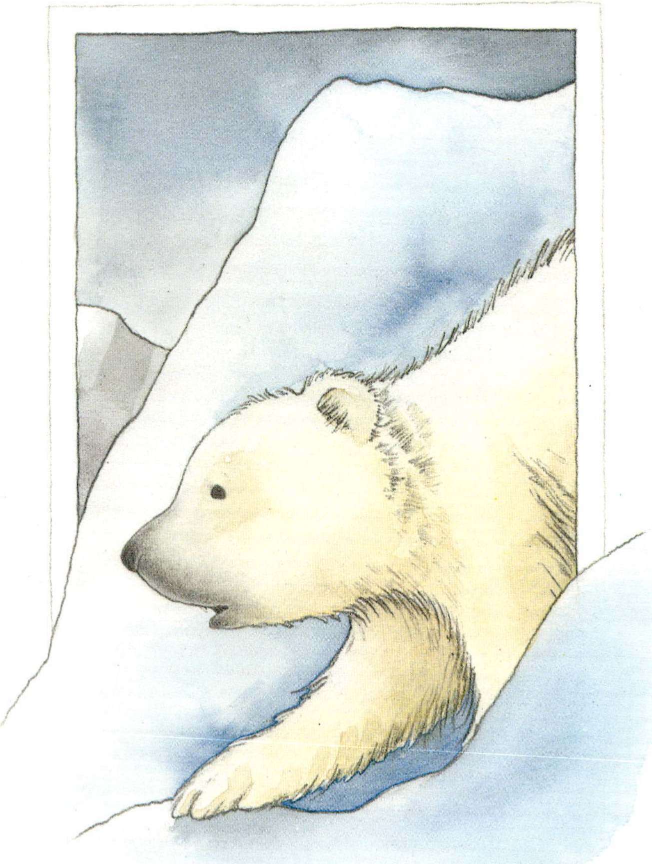

But it wasn't a seal. For one thing, the creature was much too big. For another, it had huge white tusks. Although Polo did not know it, the creature was a walrus.

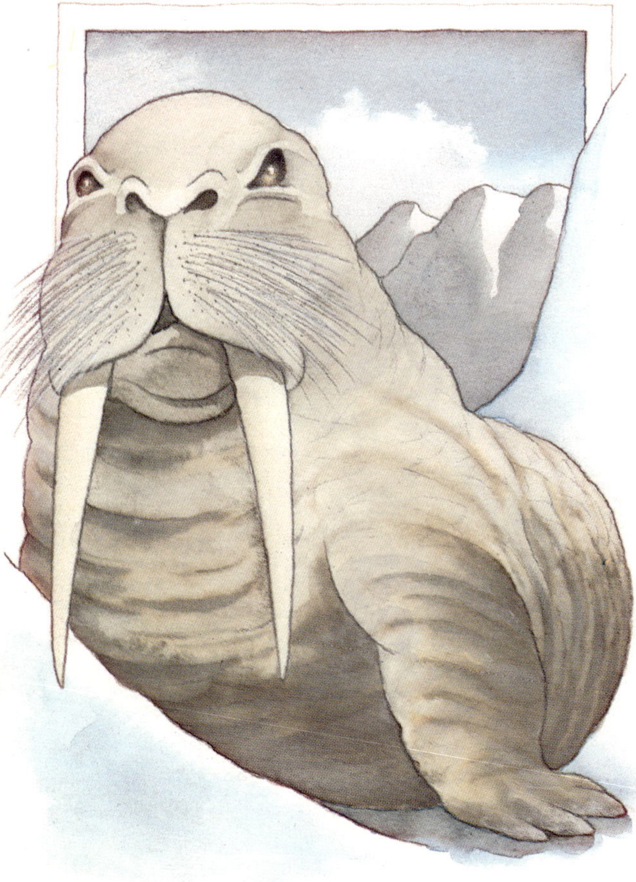

The little bear ran in fright. He ran so fast that he did not know where he was going. Suddenly, a channel of sea water loomed up ahead. Polo jumped across.

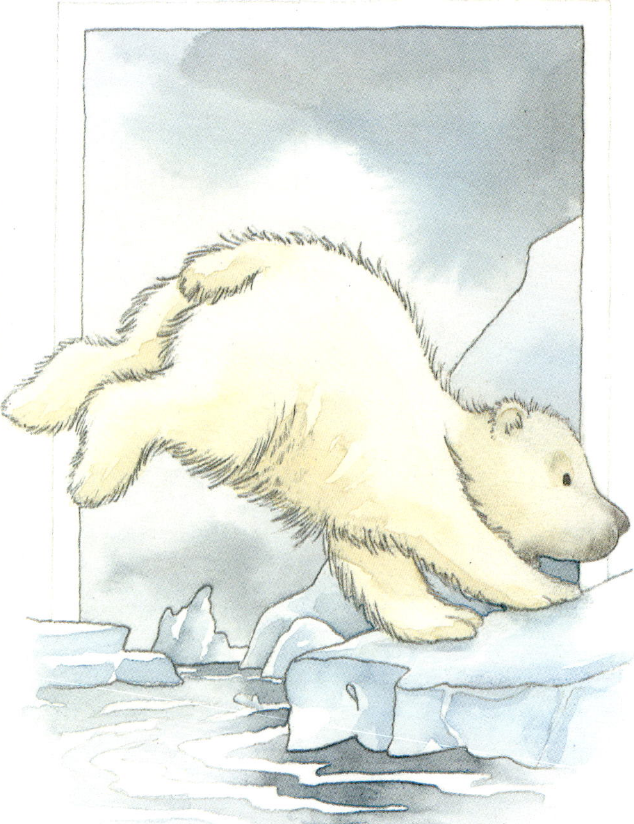

The ice moved beneath him.
It seemed to be floating out to sea.
Polo was stranded on an iceberg,
and he called out loudly for help.

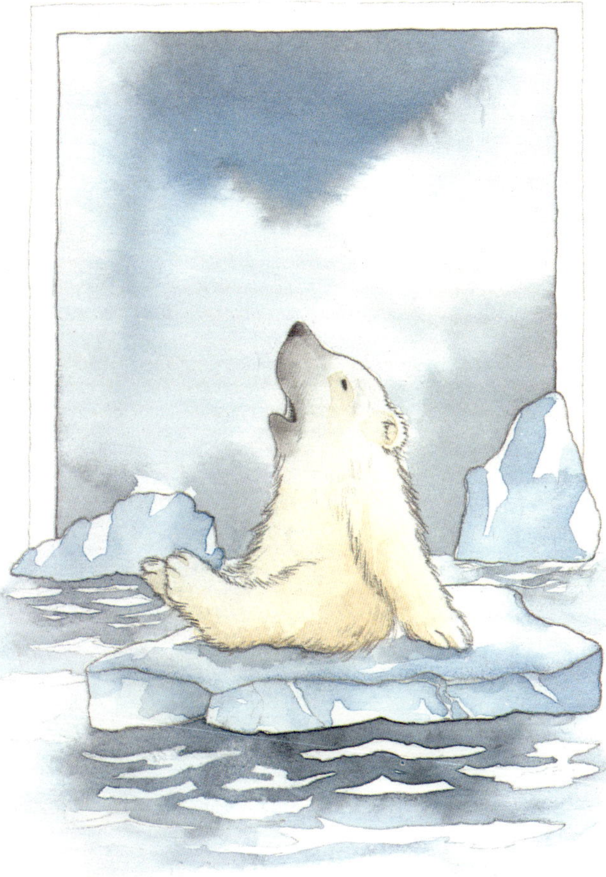

Mother bear heard his cries.
"Stay where you are!" she called
out. "Stay just where you are!"
Then she ran to the sea's edge
and plunged in.

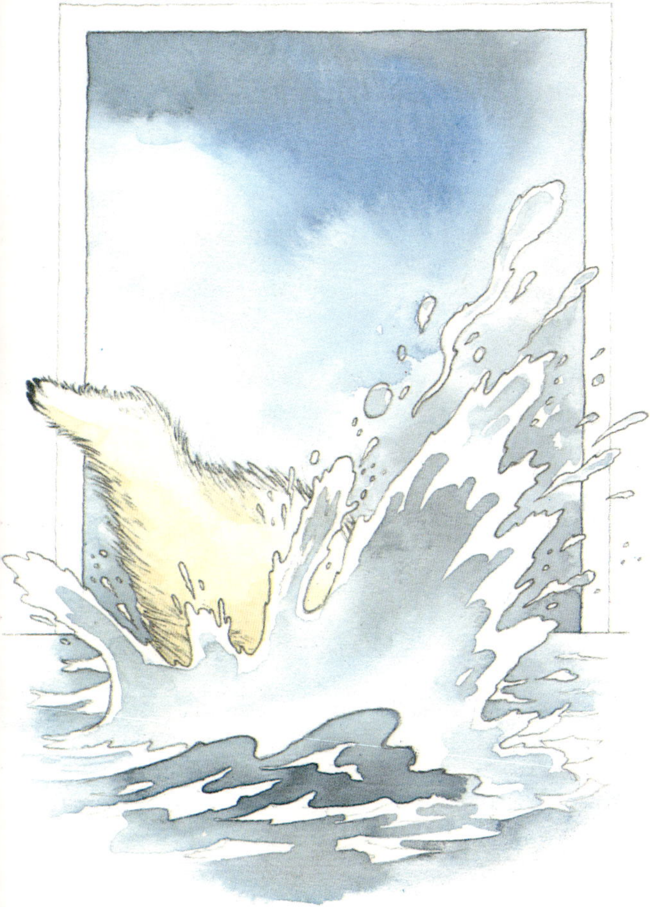

Mother bear swam to the iceberg, moving powerfully through the water.
"Climb onto my back, Polo," she called when she arrived.

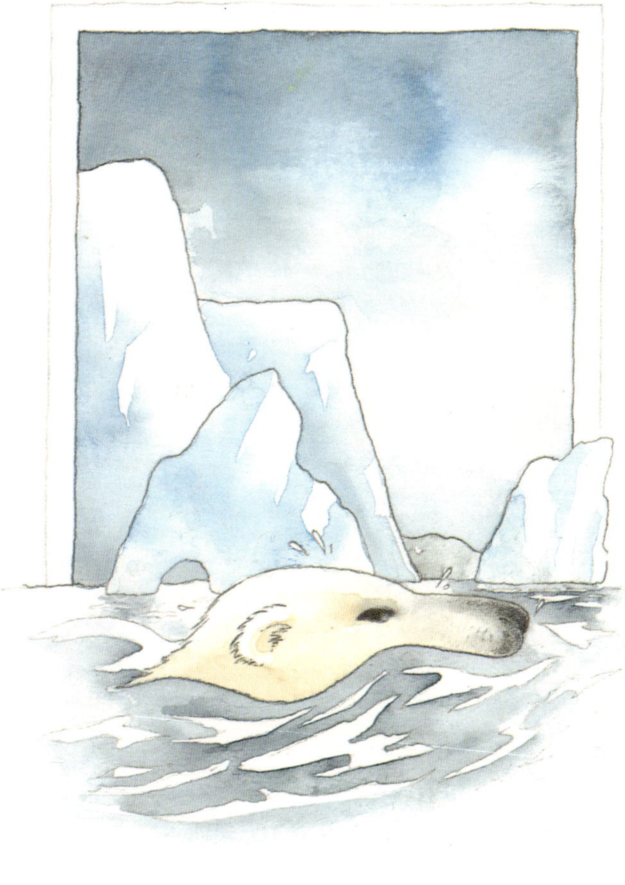

The little bear clambered down
to his mother and clung tight
as she swam back to the shore.

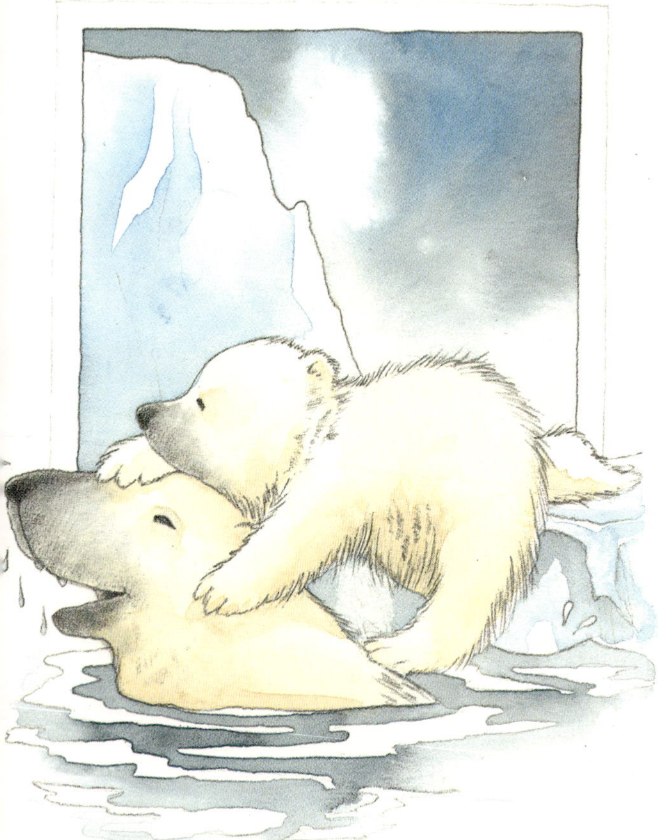

When they reached safety,
they both shook their coats to get rid
of the water. Polo knew now that
he had met danger.

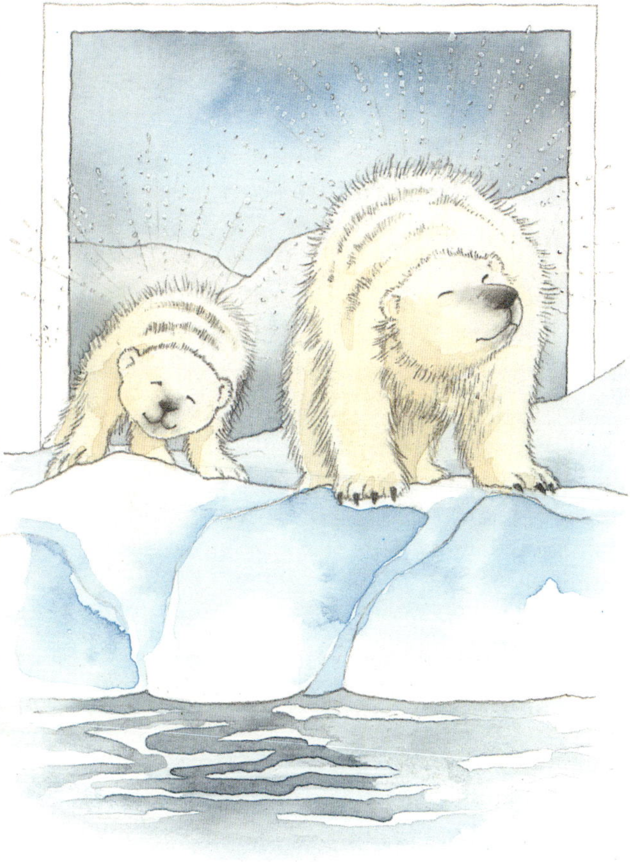

But he soon became cheerful again. "What creatures are those?" he asked, spying strange new shapes moving among the ice floes.

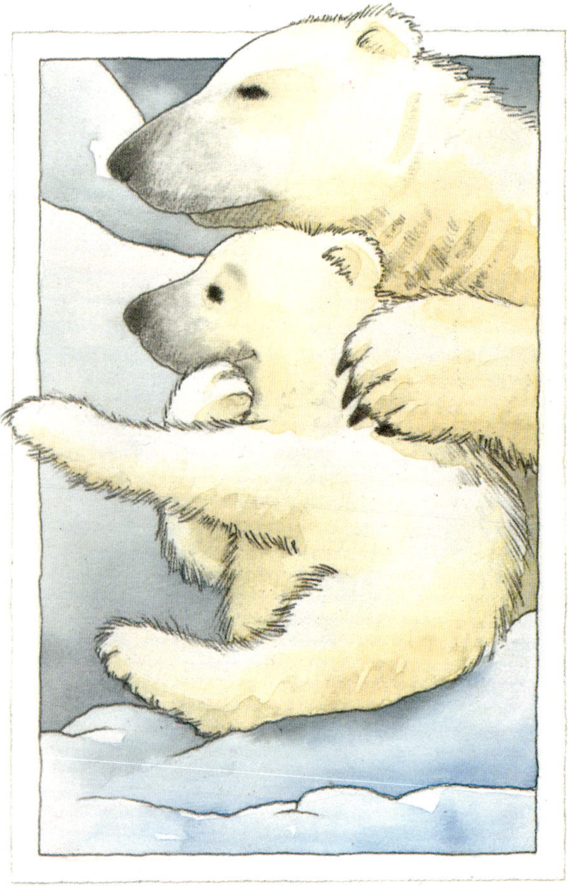

Mother pressed herself flat against the ice and told Polo to do the same. Neither of them moved a muscle. From a distance, the colour of their fur so matched the whiteness around that they could hardly be seen.

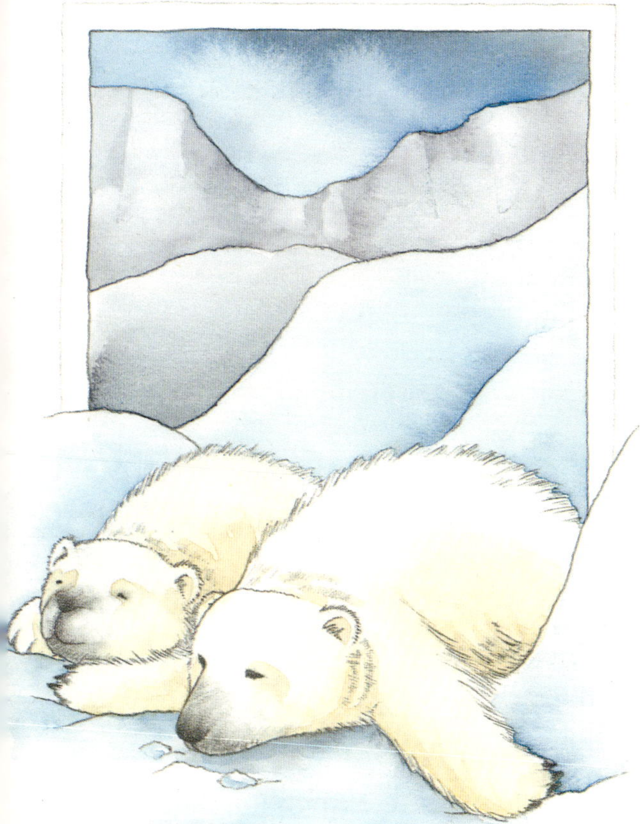

Mother and cub watched in silence as the hunters moved past in their boats.

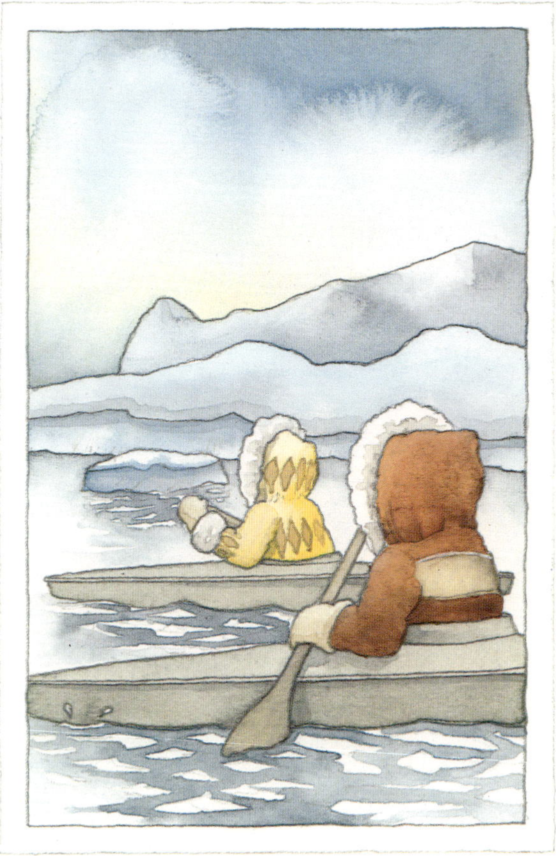

"Stay close to me, Polo," said mother bear, when she was quite sure that the hunters had gone. "You have seen enough danger for one day."

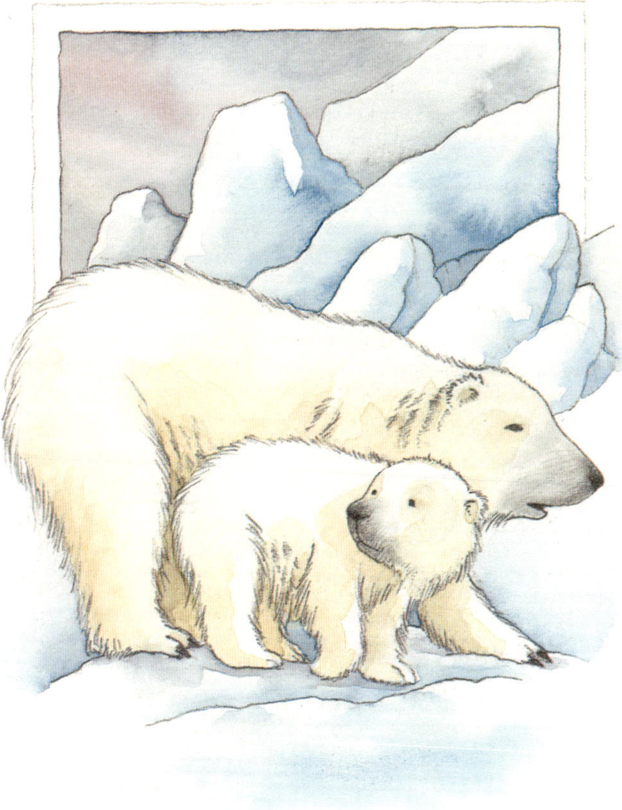

MY ROUND-THE-WORLD LIBRARY

First Edition Copyright © 1987
The Reader's Digest Association Limited,
Berkeley Square House, Berkeley Square,
London W1X 6AB

Reprinted 1990

Copyright © 1987
The Reader's Digest Association
Far East Limited

All rights reserved

® READER'S DIGEST, THE DIGEST and
the Pegasus logo are registered trademarks of
The Reader's Digest Association, Inc.
of Pleasantville, New York, U.S.A.

Printed in Hong Kong